PIRATES
WITHDRAWN

Peter Chrisp

KINGFISHER
NEW YORK

KINGFISHER
LONDON & NEW YORK

Copyright © Kingfisher 2011
Published in the United States by Kingfisher,
175 Fifth Ave., New York, NY 10010
Kingfisher is an imprint of Macmillan Children's Books, London.
All rights reserved.

Distributed in the U.S. by Macmillan,
175 Fifth Ave., New York, NY 10010

In memory of Steve Weston

Illustrations by: Linden Artists—Roger Stewart, Steve Weston,
Steve Stone (represented by Artist Partners Ltd.)

Library of Congress Cataloging-in-Publication data has been applied for.

ISBN: 978-0-7534-6611-7

Kingfisher books are available for special promotions and premiums.
For details contact: Special Markets Department, Macmillan, 175 Fifth Ave., New York, NY 10010.

For more information, please visit www.kingfisherbooks.com

Printed in China
1 3 5 7 9 8 6 4 2

1TR/0511/UG/WKT/140MA

Note to readers: The website addresses listed in this book are correct at the time of publishing.
However, due to the ever-changing nature of the Internet, website addresses and content can change.
Websites can contain links that are unsuitable for children. The publisher cannot be held responsible for
changes in website addresses or content or for information obtained through third-party websites.
We strongly advise that Internet searches should be supervised by an adult.

The Publisher would like to thank the following for permission to reproduce their material. Every care has been taken to trace copyright holders. However, if there have been unintentional omissions or failure to trace copyright holders, we apologize and will, if informed, endeavor to make corrections in any future edition (t = top, b = bottom, c = center, r = right, l = left):

Cover: tr Shutterstock/Vaide Seskauskiene; coverlc Shutterstock/Sinisa Botas; coverlb Shutterstock/Triff; coverrc Shutterstock/RCPPHOTO; Back Cover: Shutterstock/James Steidl.

Pages 4c Corbis/Joel W. Rogers; 5tr British Museum; 5c Press Association/AP; 7cl Alamy/Imagebroker; 7br Alamy/David Robertson; 8cr Alamy/Art Archive; 9tr Alamy/PCL; 10tl Werner Forman Archive (WFA)/Statens Historiska Museet, Stockholm; 10tr AKG/Imperial Treasury, Vienna; 10c WFA/National Museum Copenhagen; 11 Shutterstock/Alfio Ferlito; 12bl Bridgeman Art Library (BAL)/Claydon House, National Trust/John Hammond; 12tl BAL/Russell-Cotes Art Gallery; 12cr The Art Archive; 12br Art Archive/Topkapi Palace Museum/Dagli Orti; 13 Shutterstock/Piotr Tomicki; 13bl NGS/Topkapi Palace Museum/James L. Stanfield; 14bl Art Archive/naval Historical Museum, Venice/Dagli Orti; 16tr Shutterstock/Myotis; 16br Shutterstock/Mariano Heluani; 17 Corbis/Joel W. Rogers; 17tr BAL/NGS; 17br Art Archive/Plymouth Art Gallery/Eileen Tweedy; 18tr National Maritime Museum, Greenwich; 18br Alamy/Alexander McClearn; 19cl Alamy/Interfoto; 21tl National Geographic Society Images; 23cr National Geographic Society Images; 25t Shutterstock/movit; 25tl Shutterstock/Alex Staroseltsev; 25tr Science Photo Library/ Gary G. Gibson; 25cr BAL/Delaware Art Museum, Wilmington; 25b Shutterstock/Pablo H. Caridad; 25bl Shutterstock/Hilsom Silviu; 25br Shutterstock/Cynthia Burkhardt; 26bl AKG/Touchstone Pictures; 26cb AKG/Touchstone Pictures; 26cr AKG/Touchstone Pictures; 27tl Shutterstock/KSPhotography; 27tr Shutterstock/3drenderings; 27cr Shutterstock/Crok Photography; 27br Shutterstock/Darko Kovacevic; 28–29 Shutterstock/Mikhail; 28cr DK Images/Tina Chambers; 28bl BAL/Peter Newark; 29tr NGS/Bill Curtsinger; 29cl Shutterstock/bonsai; 29c Shutterstock/James Steidl; 29cr Shutterstock/Luba V. Nel; 29br BAL/Peter Newark; 29b Shutterstock/Pavel Vakhrushev; 30tl Alamy/Northwind Picture Archives; 30c Alamy/Matt Purciel; 31tc BAL/Peter Newark's Pictures; 31bc BAL/Peter Newark's Pictures; 32cr BAL/Peter Newark's Pictures; 34c BAL/Sir John Soane's Museum; 35tr Getty/Hulton Archive; 36–37 National Maritime Museum, Hong Kong; 36cr Corbis/Carl & Ann Purcell; 37tr BAL/Peter Newark's Pictures; 37bl Alamy/Tom Nebbia; 38tr National Maritime Museum, Greenwich; 39tc National Maritime Museum, Greenwich; 39cl BAL/Peter Newark's Pictures; 39cr National Maritime Museum, Greenwich; 40 Rex Features/Disney/David Buchan; 40c Rex Features/Disney/Everett; 40br AKG/Disney; 41tl AKG images; 41tr Kobal/Disney/RKO; 41c AKG/Universal Studios/Jasin Boland; 41br Press Association/PA; 42tl Shutterstock/Irina Tischenko; 42cl NGS/Michael Lewis; 42cr NGS/Bill Curtsinger; 43tr NGS/Bill Curtsinger; 43bl NGS/Brian Skerry; 43br Jo Atherton/Oak Island Archive; 48tr Art Archive/Laurie Platt Winfrey; 48cl Corbis/Reuters; 48cr Shutterstock/Laszlo Szirtesi; 48bl Alamy/Marco Cristofori.

CONTENTS

PIRATE SEAS

When we hear the word "pirate," we think of an eccentric character with a wooden leg, waving a cutlass and shouting phrases such as "Hoist the Jolly Roger, me hearties!" We get this idea from movies and stories. Real-life pirates are less glamorous. Pirates are simply thieves who commit crimes at sea. There have been pirates for as long as there have been seafarers, and they have sailed all of the world's oceans.

powder horn, to carry gunpowder for the pistol

flintlock pistol, used by European pirates in the 1700s

replica of the Golden Hinde, a galleon sailed by the English privateer Sir Francis Drake

This chart of the world's oceans shows where pirates have sailed throughout history.

5

4

Setting sail

Throughout history, pirates have used different types of ships to attack and plunder their victims. The earliest pirates, in the ancient Mediterranean Sea, sailed in galleys—fast ships powered by many oarsmen. Modern-day pirates, off the coast of Somalia in Africa, use small motorboats. On this map, you can see the various types of ships used by the world's most notorious pirates.

GALLEON–a large, three-masted sailing ship, with square sails and two or more decks

SPEEDY SHIPS

Pirate ships have always been faster and better armed than the vessels they prey upon in order to launch surprise attacks. Merchant ships are usually large in order to carry as many goods as possible. However, they are manned with small crews, which makes them easy to capture by pirates.

ancient Greek cup, showing a fast warship attacking a slow merchant ship

Somali pirates use motorboats to attack at high speeds

divider and compass—navigational tools used to sail the seas

KEY

1 c. 700–67 B.C.—pirates from Greece and Asia Minor (Turkey) rowed galleys called biremes

2 A.D. 793–1066—Scandinavian pirates, called Vikings, raided Europe in longships

3 1500s–1800s—North African Muslim seafarers raided Europe in galleys

4 1500s—English privateers set sail in galleons, to attack Spanish ships in the Americas

5 1650–1720—English, French, and Dutch pirates, based in the Caribbean, set off in galleons

6 1800s—Chinese pirates terrorized the South China Sea, in great fleets of junks

7 2000s—Somali pirates use motorboats to capture ships and hold them for ransom

www.nmm.ac.uk/explore/sea-and-ships/facts/ships-and-seafarers/pirates

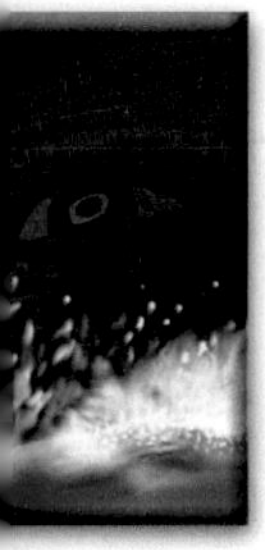

ANCIENT PIRATES

The first pirates we know of sailed the Mediterranean Sea, around the coasts of Greece and Asia Minor (Turkey), from the 700s B.C. These ancient pirates used fast, oared warships, called biremes, to attack slower-moving merchant ships. They also raided coastal settlements to take captives in order to sell them as slaves. No single state was strong enough to stop them.

BIREME—*a warship with two sets of oars on each side*

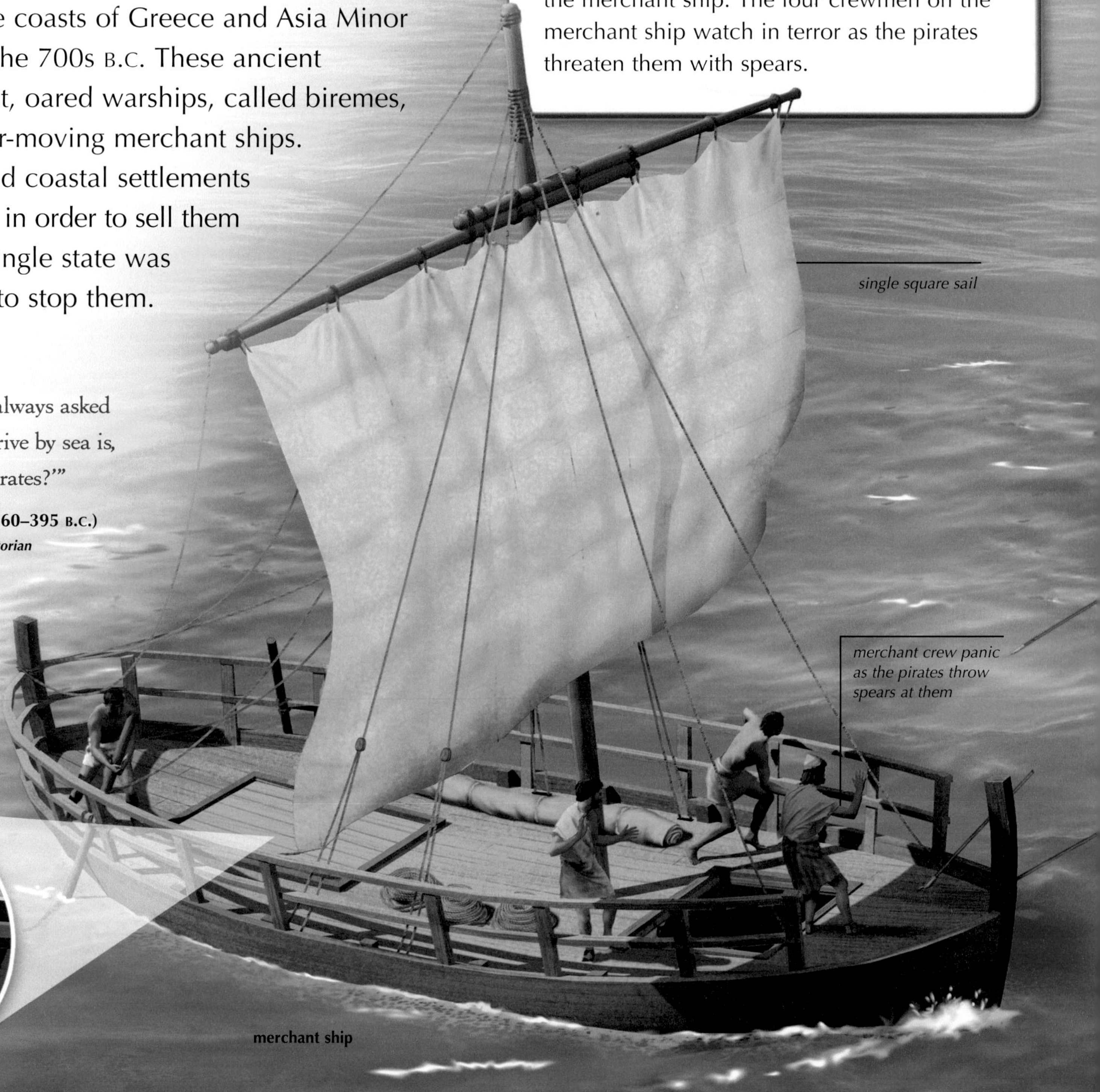

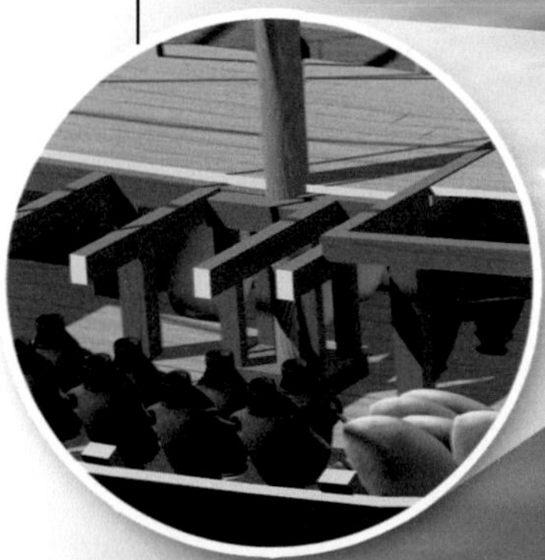

On the attack!

Lying in wait, concealed in an inlet on the island of Cyprus, pirates have seen a passing merchant ship on its way to the port of Kyrenia. The pirates rush to attack, pulling at their oars to bear down at great speed on the merchant ship. The four crewmen on the merchant ship watch in terror as the pirates threaten them with spears.

"The question always asked of those who arrive by sea is, 'Are you pirates?'"

Thucydides (c. 460–395 B.C.)
Greek historian

single square sail
merchant crew panic as the pirates throw spears at them
merchant ship

amphorae (vases) of wine, stacked in rows

The word "pirate" is Greek in origin, from *peiran*, meaning "to attack."

Slave market

The biggest slave market in the Mediterranean was on the Greek island of Delos. On a single day, up to 10,000 slaves might be sold there.

decorative, curved sternpost

two sets of oars, one above the other

pirate bireme

bronze-tipped beak, used to ram other ships

⊜ KYRENIA SHIPWRECK

In 1967, divers off Kyrenia, in Cyprus, discovered the 2,300-year-old wreck of a Greek merchant ship. The vessel's main cargo was wine from the island of Rhodes, stored in more than 400 amphorae. We know that the ship carried a crew of four, because four wooden spoons and four drinking cups were also found on board. Stuck in the hull, there were eight iron spearheads. This shows that the ship had been attacked, probably by pirates. Perhaps the four crewmen were taken by pirates and sold as slaves.

wreck on show in the Kyrenia Museum

▼ RANSOM—*money raised for the release of a captive*

Julius Caesar

In 75 B.C., a young Roman nobleman named Julius Caesar was captured by Cilician pirates, who demanded a ransom of 20 talents (1,430 lb./ 650kg) of silver. Caesar burst out laughing, saying they did not realize how important a man he was. He offered to pay 50 talents instead but also promised that he would later have all the pirates crucified.

Caesar thought that the Cilician pirates were foolish and treated them with scorn.

"The power of the pirates stretched over the whole Mediterranean Sea."

Plutarch (c. A.D. 46–120)
Greek historian, from his Life of Pompey

CILICIAN PIRATES

In 100 B.C., Cilicia, in what is now southern Turkey, was a major pirate stronghold. Cilician pirates were a menace across the Mediterranean, attacking coastal towns and seizing ships. They also made fortunes by taking high-ranking captives and holding them for ransom. This brought them into conflict with the Romans, who were becoming the most powerful people in the whole of the Mediterranean at that time. The Romans were determined to crush the Cilician pirates.

Caesar's revenge

Caesar sent messengers to various places to raise the ransom sum, in Greek silver coins. After being freed, Caesar collected some warships and returned to capture the pirates. He caught them by surprise while their ships were at anchor. Caesar had them crucified, just as he had promised he would.

 ➤ The Romans called the Mediterranean *mare nostrum*, which means "our sea."

Roman Empire

The Roman Empire (red on map) came to include all the lands around the Mediterranean Sea. By depriving pirates of land bases, the Romans were able to put a stop to piracy.

⊖ PIRATE STRONGHOLD

The last Cilician pirate stronghold was a rocky headland called Coracesium. It was there that Pompey fought and won a great sea battle against a huge pirate fleet. He then captured Coracesium, taking 20,000 prisoners. But instead of executing them, he resettled them in lands away from the sea, where they could become farmers.

Coracesium, today called Alanya

Pompey

By 67 B.C., the pirates of Cilicia had become such a problem to Rome that Pompey, a leading general, was granted special powers to fight a war against them. His force included a fleet of 500 ships, plus 120,000 infantry (foot soldiers) and 5,000 cavalry (soldiers on horseback). In just three months, Pompey defeated most of the pirates.

corvus (crow)—
a bridge lowered to
board enemy ships

Pompey gives orders
to his officers

**Roman naval bireme
(a ship with two
banks of oars)**

A VIKING RAID

In the year 793, sea raiders from Scandinavia, called Vikings, sailed across the North Sea and raided the monastery of Lindisfarne in northeast England. A monastery was a place where Christian holy men, called monks, spent their lives in prayer. They were ideal places for Vikings to attack because they were usually close to the sea and they were filled with treasures. The monks were peace-loving people with no weapons.

> LONGSHIP—a Viking warship with a long, narrow hull, powered by oars and a square sail

● WAR GOD

Viking carving, in memory of a dead warrior

No Christians would dream of attacking a monastery. But the Vikings were not Christians. They worshiped violent gods such as Odin, god of war. Vikings believed that warriors who died in battle would go to feast with Odin in his drinking hall, Valhalla. This carving shows Odin's eight-legged horse, Sleipnir (Slippy), riding toward Valhalla carrying either the god or a dead warrior. In the lower panel, a band of Vikings sail a longship.

Vikings gave their swords names, such as "leg biter."

A battleax from a Viking warrior's grave in Denmark.

Monk's treasure

A monastery's treasures included Bibles with jeweled covers. To a Viking, this Bible was not a holy book but a source of wealth.

Surprise attack

The terrified monks of Lindisfarne have no chance against the Vikings, who charge toward them, waving swords and battleaxes. Some of the Vikings carry away the monastery's treasures. Others are dragging captured monks toward their longships. They will take these prisoners back home to Norway to sell them as thralls (slaves).

Viking longships had dragon figureheads.

Vikings arriving on the shores of Lindisfarne

Longships, light enough to be dragged up onto a beach, were perfect pirate vessels.

A chest served as an oarsman's seat and also held his belongings.

"Never before has such terror appeared in Britain nor was it thought possible that such an attack from the sea could be made!"

Bishop Alcuin of York (c. A.D. 735–804)

⟩ Ships were so important to Vikings that their rulers were sometimes buried in them.

www.viking.no/e/index.html

BARBARY CORSAIRS

From the 1500s to the 1800s, North African Muslim seafarers, called Barbary corsairs, terrorized the coasts of Europe. From their bases in the ports of Algiers, Tripoli, and Tunis, they set sail to raid European shipping and coastal settlements. Their main aim was to seize slaves. In all, the corsairs are thought to have captured more than one million Europeans, who ended up as slaves in North Africa.

Ransom

In Europe, there were special groups of friars (religious men dedicated to Christianity) set up with the main purpose of raising money to free captured Europeans from slavery.

Turning Turk

In the early 1600s, Englishmen and Dutchmen joined the corsairs. Sir Francis Verney (1584–1616) was a young nobleman fleeing debts and an unhappy marriage in England. In North Africa, he converted to Islam and became a corsair. Such behavior shocked other Europeans, who called it "turning Turk."

Slaves

The captives ended up in Muslim slave markets, such as this one in Istanbul. They were forced to work as household servants, as laborers in fields and quarries, and as oarsmen in the corsairs' galleys. To prevent them from escaping, galley slaves were locked up at night, in prisons called bagnos.

BARBAROSSA

The most famous corsair was Kheir-ed-Din (c. 1478–1546), nicknamed Barbarossa (Red Beard). In the 1520s and 1530s, he sacked many ports in Italy and France and captured several Greek islands. Barbarossa was so successful that he rose to become pasha (governor) of Algiers and chief admiral of the Turkish fleet. This painting shows him as an old man, when his beard had turned white.

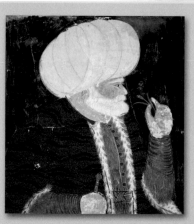

portrait of Barbarossa

> In 1631, almost all the inhabitants of Baltimore, an Irish village, were captured by Barbary corsairs.

> "Galleys can only be worked by pitiless cruelty toward the slaves."

Jean Marteilhe
ex-galley slave, 1757

Janissaries

Every corsair ship carried between 70 and 150 professional warriors, called janissaries. They came from Turkey and central Europe, where, as children, they were recruited into special military schools. There, they learned to fight using a musket and sword. They were also taught to see themselves as holy warriors fighting for the religion of Islam.

saif—an Arab slashing sword with a curved blade

Galleys

Corsairs sailed in galleys—fast ships that were rowed into battle by slaves, who sat chained to benches below decks. For long journeys, they used sail power. Each galley had a single mast with a large lateen (triangular) sail.

purple sash (from the Arabic word shash*) worn as a belt*

elaborately detailed scabbard

A CORSAIR GALLEY

Barbary corsairs used a powerful warship, called a galley, that was designed for frontal attack. Unlike a galleon, with cannon arranged along the sides, the galley's firepower was in the bow (front). Attacking front-on meant that a galley presented a more narrow target to enemy gunfire than a broad-sided galleon. Each galley carried up to 250 oarsmen, between 80 and 150 janissaries (soldiers), and a small crew of sailors to handle the large sail.

Preparing to sail

The harbor of Algiers bustles with activity as the Barbary corsairs prepare to set off on a raiding expedition. Slave oarsmen take their places on the benches, and the heavily armed janissaries stroll on board. Supplies of food and water are also assembled. Each oarsmen must drink half a gallon of water a day to prevent him from passing out from heat and exhaustion.

Rais

The rais, or the captain, is in complete command of the galley at sea. This rais is an Englishman who has "turned Turk" (see page 12). He knows the seas around Europe and the best places to raid for slaves.

⊘ SAILING SHIPS

In the 1600s, the corsairs began to build sailing ships as well as galleys. Without the many oarsmen to feed, the corsairs could now go on much longer expeditions. They sailed out into the Atlantic Ocean—as far as the British Isles, Iceland, and Newfoundland—raiding for slaves.

sailing ship, with lateen (triangular) sails

> Europeans also sailed galleys in the Mediterranean, using prisoners and captured Muslims as oarsmen.

Janissary

The janissaries play no part in the work of sailing the ship. They simply lounge around on deck, smoking pipes, until it is time to fire the cannon, storm another ship, or raid a coastal village.

Slave oarsman

The slaves sit side by side, chained to benches, three or more pulling a single, huge oar. They live on a diet of ship's biscuits and water. Their one hope of freedom is that the galley will be captured in battle.

Slave driver

The slave driver patrols the deck with a whip, lashing those who do not pull hard enough. If a slave can no longer row, he will be thrown overboard. The slave driver is the most hated man on board the galley.

harbor of Algiers

NEW WORLD

In the 1500s, the Spaniards conquered an empire in the Americas. These lands were found to be rich in silver and gold. From the "New World," as Europeans called the Americas, Spanish galleons shipped huge amounts of treasure back to Europe. For enemies of Spain, such as the English sea captain Francis Drake, these treasure galleons provided a perfect opportunity for plunder.

PLUNDER—to steal goods from a place, often during a war

Spanish loot

Treasure galleons from Spain carried cargoes of gold coins, called doubloons, and silver coins, called dollars. These dollars were nicknamed "pieces of eight," because each was worth eight smaller coins, called reals.

breastplate worn over doublet (jacket)

sword with an elaborate hilt, protecting the hand

The *Golden Hinde*

In 1578, Drake sailed into the Pacific Ocean on board the *Golden Hinde*, a small ship about 100 ft. (30m) long. Off the coast of South America, he captured a Spanish galleon loaded with treasure. The Spaniards did not expect to find English ships in the Pacific Ocean. They assumed the *Golden Hinde* was a Spanish ship, until Drake suddenly opened fire on them.

Francis Drake

Privateers were people who were given government permission to rob enemy ships and lands, and England's Francis Drake (1540–1596) was a famous example. In 1577, Queen Elizabeth I sent him to plunder the Spanish Americas, in exchange for half the booty.

Drake's ship carried nine large cannon, like this, and several smaller ones.

"I pray for England's sake: the Lord preserve the noble Drake."

Thomas Greepe
ballad writer, 1587

> The galleon captured by Francis Drake carried so much treasure that it took six days to move it to the *Golden Hinde*.

modern replica of the *Golden Hinde*

one of the ship's five square sails

⊖ DRAKE REWARDED

In 1580, Drake returned home after a three-year voyage, having sailed all the way around the world. Queen Elizabeth I was so pleased with her half share of his booty that she decided to make Drake a knight. For the next 100 years, the *Golden Hinde* was preserved in London, England, as a national monument, until the ship finally rotted away. Two replicas of the ship exist today.

Queen Elizabeth I knights Drake on board the *Golden Hinde*

Drake's drum

This drum belonged to Drake, who had it beaten on board the *Golden Hinde* to send his men to battle stations. It is kept at Drake's home, Buckland Abbey, in Devon, England. According to legend, in times of great national danger Drake's drum magically makes a rumbling sound, to warn the nation.

BUCCANEERS OF TORTUGA

MUSKET—a shoulder gun with a long barrel, whose bore (inside shaft) is smooth

In the 1600s, the French settled on the northwest coast of Hispaniola (Haiti), where they hunted wild cattle and pigs. They smoked this meat over a wooden frame, called a boucan. They came to be nicknamed "buccaneers." The Spaniards drove these buccaneers out of Hispaniola in about 1630. They settled on the little island of Tortuga, which they turned into a pirate base, to attack Spanish settlements and ships.

Cutlass

Buccaneers were armed with a short sword with a slightly curved blade, called a cutlass. It was perfect for fighting at close quarters on board a ship.

cutlass and scabbard (sword sheath)

Sloops

The buccaneers used little, single-masted ships called sloops, which could be rowed as well as sailed. Their small size allowed buccaneers to lurk in shallow inlets, waiting for passing ships to attack.

A pole, called a gaff, supports the main sail.

🔘 TURTLE ISLAND

Tortuga is Spanish for "turtle," a name suggested by the island's humpy shape, similar to a turtle's shell. With a steep, rocky coastline and only a single harbor, protected by a fort, Tortuga made the perfect pirate stronghold. The buccaneers who settled there called themselves the "Brotherhood of the Coast."

painting of Tortuga in the 1600s, showing its harbor and fort

François L'Ollonais (c. 1635–1668)
French buccaneer

*musket was up to 5 ft.
(1.5m) in length*

François L'Ollonais

The most famous buccaneer
was the cruel François L'Ollonais
(c. 1635–1668). As a young man,
he had been shipwrecked off
the coast of Mexico, where
Spanish soldiers killed most of
his shipmates. L'Ollonais swore
to torture and kill any Spaniard he
could capture by way of revenge.

Seizing a ship

Buccaneers were skilled marksmen, thanks to their
experience hunting wild pigs and cattle. Their
main weapon was a musket with a long barrel,
called a *fusil boucanier*. When attacking a ship,
they first opened fire on the men on deck,
forcing them to take cover below. Once
the decks were cleared, the buccaneers
boarded and seized the ship.

*cutlass used in hand-
to-hand fighting*

PIRATE CAPITAL

In 1655, the English seized the Caribbean island of Jamaica from Spain. To defend Jamaica, the government invited British buccaneers to settle there, around the strongly defended harbor of Port Royal. From this base, the buccaneers set out to attack Spanish settlements and shipping in the Americas. Although England's war with Spain ended in 1660, the buccaneer raids continued. The lawless port was later described as "the wickedest city in the world."

SACK—to plunder a town after capturing it, burning buildings and taking away valuables

Bustling port

By 1670, Port Royal was one of the largest English settlements in the Americas. The town included churches, stores, waterfront warehouses, and large houses owned by wealthy merchants. There were also places of entertainment, including gambling houses and taverns. About half of the population of 4,000 earned a living from the raids against the Spaniards.

clay pipes, made using molds

17th-century bottles of rum

1

2

3

 Henry Morgan lives on today as the name of a famous brand of Jamaican rum, called Captain Morgan.

Earthquake!

In 1692, Port Royal was hit by a terrible earthquake, in which most of the town disappeared beneath the waves. This disaster was described by preachers as a punishment sent by God.

⊜ HENRY MORGAN

The best-known buccaneer in Port Royal was a Welshman named Henry Morgan. Between 1667 and 1671, he led four large expeditions to the mainland, sacking four Spanish towns. The raids were illegal, as England was not at war with Spain. But, rather than punishing him, King Charles II gave Morgan a knighthood and made him governor of Jamaica.

Sir Henry Morgan

http://nautarch.tamu.edu/portroyal

Port Royal, Jamaica,
in 1670

KEY

1 Rich merchant and his wife

2 Tavern, where buccaneers drink Jamaican rum

3 Store selling clay pipes

4 Two drunken buccaneers

5 House, made of timber and brick

6 Ship, part of a fleet commanded by Henry Morgan

7 Unloading goods looted from a Spanish settlement

GUN PORT—*a small opening in the side of the ship, through which a cannon is fired*

A PIRATE SHIP

Pirate ships had to be fast, well-armed, and able to withstand rough weather. They were usually captured merchant ships, converted for war. Pirates cut extra gun ports in the sides of the hull to take cannon. They often removed deck structures, such as cabins, creating a continuous fighting platform. One of the best known is Blackbeard's ship, *Queen Anne's Revenge*, whose wreck was discovered in 1996.

hand grenades, packed with gunpowder

Blackbeard's ship

In 1717, English pirates, led by Benjamin Hornigold, captured the French slave ship *La Concorde* off Martinique. Hornigold gave the ship to one of his men, Edward Teach, nicknamed Blackbeard. He renamed it *Queen Anne's Revenge* and fitted it with 40 cannon. Blackbeard sailed *Queen Anne's Revenge* from the west coast of Africa to the Caribbean and the east coast of North America.

cannon, mounted on wheeled carriages, to be rolled forward for firing

> Under Blackbeard's command, *Queen Anne's Revenge* took at least 18 ships as prizes.

◉ THE DISCOVERY

The *Queen Anne's Revenge* was one of the largest pirate ships, and it was her size that was her downfall. In 1718, she ran aground while trying to enter Beaufort Inlet off North Carolina. Blackbeard abandoned ship, taking most of his treasure. In 1996, divers discovered the wreck. Thousands of artifacts have been recovered, including anchors, grenades, and navigational equipment.

underwater anchor

Blackbeard's dividers

These are the dividers from *Queen Anne's Revenge*, used to plot a course on a chart— perhaps by Blackbeard himself!

Blackbeard's ship at sea, with the cannon ready to fire a broadside (see page 26)

www.ncmaritimemuseums.com

"Blackbeard has a ship of 40-odd guns under him."

Robert Johnson (1682–1735)
governor of South Carolina, May 1718

ELECT—to select someone for a job by voting for them

LIFE AT SEA

Although a pirate's life was dangerous, it was often more attractive than the lives of sailors on naval or merchant ships. While sailors were strictly disciplined, and flogged for minor offenses, there were no floggings on pirate ships. Everyone had a say in big decisions, and captains were elected by the men. There was less work to do because pirates carried larger crews than merchant vessels. There was also the opportunity to get rich quick.

> "A merry life and a short one shall be my motto."
>
> **Bartholomew Roberts (1682–1722)**
> *Welsh Captain and pirate*

pewter tankards for drinking rum

Carousing

With no discipline and plenty of free time, pirates spent many hours drinking rum or any other alcoholic beverages that they could get hold of. Pirates also loved music and song, and there was always someone on board who could play a fiddle.

> Bartholomew Roberts had a band of musicians on his ship, whose job was to entertain the men.

"*Every man has a vote in affairs of moment; has equal title to the fresh provisions, or strong liquors, at any time seized. To desert the ship or their quarters in battle, is punished with death or marooning. No striking one another on board, but every man's quarrels to be ended on shore, at sword and pistol. No man to talk of breaking up their way of living, till each had shared one thousand pounds. Each man shall keep his piece, cutlass, and pistols at all times clean and ready for action.*"

Rules for living

Pirates often drew up a set of rules, called articles, which everybody had to agree to follow. Every crewman signed the articles, but if they could not write they would make a mark, such as a cross, on the document. These are some of Captain Bartholomew Roberts' rules for his crew.

Careening

One of the perils of the Caribbean was shipworm, which ate its way through wooden hulls. Pirates had to drag their ships into secluded coves, tilt them over, and scrape off the worms. This was called careening.

⊖ MAROONING

A common pirate punishment for deserting in battle, or stealing from fellow pirates, was to maroon the offender. They would be left behind on an island or deserted coast, with a pistol, ammunition, and a little food and water. For the victim, marooning might end in a slow death from starvation.

painting of a marooned pirate

Gambling

Pirates loved to gamble with cards and dice. The trouble with gambling was that it often led to fights, with the loser accusing the winner of cheating. In some pirate articles, gambling was banned.

playing cards from the 1700s

pirates' dice were just like modern ones

PIRATE ATTACK!

Pirates aimed to take a ship without a fight. They began by running up a Jolly Roger flag, to scare their victims into surrendering. If the victims did not give in, the pirates fired their cannon and then closed in and boarded. They swarmed over the decks, shouting and brandishing cutlasses and pistols. In most cases, merchant seamen, knowing they were outnumbered, gave up at the sight of the flag.

Broadside

A pirate attack began with a broadside. The pirates fired all the cannon on one side of their ship at the target vessel, shattering its masts and ripping its sails and rigging. At this, the victims often ran below deck for cover. The pirates then drew their ship alongside the vessel, so they could board for hand-to-hand fighting.

Cutlass

The cutlass was the main weapon used in hand-to-hand fighting. Pirates did not have to be skilled at handling one, for they usually overwhelmed their victims by sheer numbers.

"... engaged with barbarous and inhuman enemies, with their black and bloody flags hanging over us, without the least appearance of ever escaping, but to be cut to pieces."

Captain James Mackrae (1670–1746)
*from a letter detailing a pirate attack
off Madagascar on November 16, 1720*

boarding the prize by swinging on a rope

sails torn by the broadside

firing a broadside

Grappling iron

When closing in, pirates threw grappling irons, which hooked onto a ship's rigging or hull, allowing them to pull it closer for boarding. Once alongside, they used axes to climb the ship's wooden sides.

Flintlock pistol

Pirates were also armed with flintlock pistols, which could fire one shot before being reloaded. They often carried several pistols, tucked into their belts. After firing, they used the butt end as a club.

hand-to-hand fighting on the deck of the prize

● THE JOLLY ROGER

A pirate flag, called a Jolly Roger, was usually black and white and always carried a frightening image, such as a skull and crossbones, a skeleton, a cutlass, or a devil. Different pirate captains had their own personal designs. The flag of the notorious Blackbeard, for example, had a skeleton with a devil's horns pointing a spear at a bleeding heart.

skull and crossbones, the best-known pirate flag

www.isd12.org/bhe/Archives/Activities/Pirates/Pages/Weapons/weapons.html

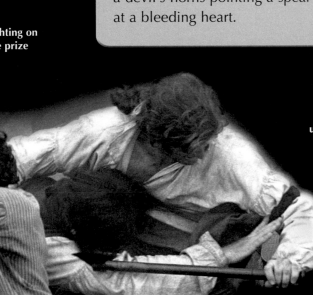

boarding ax is used as a weapon

Warning shot

If possible, pirates preferred to capture a ship without damaging it. So, before using the broadside, pirates often fired a cannon as a warning shot to one side of the prize.

MOGUL EMPIRE—a Muslim empire in India, lasting from the 1500s to the 1800s

TAKING A PRIZE

Once they had captured a prize, pirates ransacked it for treasure or anything that might be of use for their own ship. They took food, drink, ammunition, sails, and ropes, for pirates could not easily sail into a port to buy supplies. They might even decide to keep the whole ship. Merchant vessels usually carried ordinary trading goods, but if the pirates were lucky they might take a true treasure ship.

Pirates' revenge

Pirates were mostly ex-merchant seamen, and they enjoyed taking revenge on captured merchant captains. A captain accused of mistreating his crew might be whipped or even killed. Some pirates enjoyed torturing their prisoners. The cruelest was English captain Ned Low (c. 1690–c. 1724). In this engraving, one of Low's men is shooting a prisoner in the face.

Walking the plank

A common pirate punishment, familiar from movies and books, was "walking the plank." Although a rare event, it did happen occasionally. In 1822, Captain William Smith was captured by Spanish pirates and forced to walk a plank. When he reached the end, the pirates tipped him into the water and shot him as he swam.

an old seafarer's map, on parchment

Treasure chest

There is a widespread belief that pirates kept their stolen treasure in chests, which they buried on desert islands for safekeeping. This idea comes from Robert Louis Stevenson's 1883 children's novel, *Treasure Island*. The story begins with the discovery of a treasure map left by Captain Flint— "the bloodthirstiest buccaneer that ever lived." In fact, pirates always preferred to spend their wealth if they could.

> When Black Sam Bellamy's ship sank, it was carrying about 5.5 tons (5 metric tonnes) of stolen silver and gold.

Bellamy's treasure

This is a selection of just some of the gold and silver stolen by the notorious pirate Black Sam Bellamy, which he took from 53 captured ships. It was found in the wreck of his own ship, the *Whydah Galley* (see page 43), which sank in a storm off Cape Cod, Massachusetts, in 1717.

"We plunder the rich under the protection of our own courage."

Black Sam Bellamy (1689–1717)
said to a captive whom Bellamy was trying to persuade to join him

www.cindyvallar.com/treasure.html

Precious gems

In 1695, a pirate named Henry Avery captured the *Ganj-i-Sawai*, a ship belonging to the Mogul emperor of India, which was carrying pilgrims and treasure from India to Arabia. Its wealthy female passengers were adorned with jewelry, including Indian gems, which the pirates seized greedily.

● CAPTAIN KIDD

Unlike the story in *Treasure Island*, pirates rarely buried treasure. The only recorded case is that of Captain William Kidd (c. 1645–1701), a Scottish privateer accused of being a pirate. In 1698, Kidd, who believed he could prove his innocence, hid some of his treasure on Gardiner's Island, in the state of New York, before giving himself up. Soon afterward, the treasure was found and used in evidence at his trial. Kidd was found guilty and later hanged.

fanciful painting of Kidd burying his treasure

HUNTING BLACKBEARD

The most terrifying pirate of them all was Edward Teach, or Thatch, nicknamed "Blackbeard." From 1716–1718, Blackbeard plundered shipping along the east coast of America. His notorious career as a pirate ended in a famous battle, off Okracoke Island in North Carolina, against Lieutenant Robert Maynard of the British Navy. The terror of the seas was killed, but his legend lives on.

Governor of Virginia

In 1718, Alexander Spotswood, governor of Virginia, found out where Blackbeard was based. Spotswood sent Lieutenant Robert Maynard, with two sloops and 60 men, to take the pirate, dead or alive.

"Blackbeard fell with five shot in him, and 20 dismal cuts in several parts of his body."

Lieutenant Robert Maynard (1684–1751)
of the British Navy

Maynard's sword blade has broken

pistol-shot wound

Fatal fighting

The pirates board Maynard's ship, and a fierce hand-to-hand fight begins. Blackbeard and Maynard slash at each other with their swords, until Maynard's blade breaks. Just then, another sailor attacks Blackbeard from behind, gashing his neck. The pirate fights on until, in the act of cocking his pistol, he suddenly drops dead.

sailor attacks Blackbeard from behind

> FUSE—*a slow-burning piece of rope, used to fire cannon and ignite (set off) grenades*

Blackbeard made his final stand at the picturesque Okracoke Inlet.

Losing his head

Maynard chopped off Blackbeard's head and hung it from the bows of his ship, *Pearl*, bringing it back to Virginia to show Governor Spotswood that he had achieved his goal. Blackbeard's body was thrown into the sea.

● DEVIL FROM HELL

Blackbeard deliberately set out to terrify people, so they would surrender without a fight. At a time when most men were clean-shaven, he grew a long, thick, black beard, which he twisted with red ribbons. Before going into battle, he stuck burning fuses under his hat. With his naturally wild eyes, these made him look like a devil from the depths of hell. Even Blackbeard's own men were scared of him.

Blackbeard, with smoking fuses under his hat

❯ Blackbeard's head was stuck on a pole beside Chesapeake Bay, eastern U.S.A., at a site still called Blackbeard's Point today.

FEMALE PIRATES

In 1720, two years after the notorious Blackbeard's death, another pirate ship, under "Calico" Jack Rackham, was captured off the Bahamas. There was a sensation when it was revealed that two of the captured pirates were actually women! Their names were Anne Bonny and Mary Read, and both went into battle dressed as men, armed with pistols and cutlasses. They also fought more bravely than any of their shipmates, who cowered below deck when their ship was captured.

LITERARY LADIES

The astonishing story of Anne Bonny and Mary Read was told by Captain Charles Johnson, in *A General History of the Robberies & Murders of the Most Notorious Pirates*—a popular book of 1724. He collected information about the female pirates from their Jamaican trial. This illustration from the book shows the pair armed with cutlasses and boarding axes.

Anne and Mary dressed as male sailors

Anne Bonny

A red-haired Irish woman, Anne Bonny had settled with her husband in New Providence Island, in the Bahamas. This was a regular haunt of pirates, including "Calico" Jack Rackham, whose nickname came from his colorful clothing. Anne fell in love with Jack and, disguised as a man, ran away to sea with him.

Anne and Jack run away to sea

Mary Read

An English woman named Mary Read was raised as a boy by her mother. She did this to get money from her mother-in-law, who wanted to have a grandson. As an adult, Mary enlisted as a male soldier in the British Army, serving in a war in Flanders. She learned how to use weapons and to pass herself off as a man.

Mary dressed in the uniform of a British musketeer

"As to hanging, she thought it no great hardship, for, were it not for that, every cowardly fellow would turn pirate."

Mary Read (c. 1690–1721)
at her trial, according to Captain Charles Johnson's General History, 1724

> Mary Read was one of several 17th-century women who joined the British Army or Navy, posing as men.

Anne and Mary became good friends at sea

Shipmates

Still dressed as a man, Mary Read joins a ship bound for the West Indies, to seek a new life there. The ship is captured by pirates, who force her to join them. After more adventures, she joins "Calico" Jack Rackham's crew in 1720. There, she is amazed to find another woman, Anne Bonny. The two become close friends, fighting alongside each other in battle.

Captured

In October 1720, naval troops boarded Rackham's ship. Most of the male pirates hid below, in fear. On deck, Anne and Mary shouted to their crewmates to come up and fight. Mary was so angry, she fired her pistols into the hold. The troops captured the pirates.

On trial

The pirates were tried in Jamaica, and all were sentenced to death by hanging. However, Anne and Mary escaped punishment when they both revealed that they were expecting babies. While Mary died in prison, Anne's fate remains unknown.

Farewell

Before "Calico" Jack's hanging, Anne was allowed to visit him in prison and say one last goodbye. She said that she was sorry to see him there, but that if he had fought like a man, he need not have been hanged like a dog.

The tall gibbet could be
seen for miles around.

tarred body of
Captain Kidd,
hanged in 1701

ship passing
down the
Thames River
from London,
England

Crows would eat
the corpse, so it
was covered in
tar to deter them.

In prison
While awaiting trial, pirates
were held in one of London's
prisons. An 18th-century prison
was a private business, run
for profit. Prisoners had to buy
their own food and drink, and
men and women mixed freely.

The gibbet stood at
Tilbury Point, a desolate
spot on the Thames River
in London, England.

PUNISHING
PIRATES

Captured British pirates were often brought back to
London, England, to be tried. The sentence for the
guilty was, in the words used by the judge, to be
"hanged until you are dead, dead, dead. And the
Lord have mercy on your souls." Hangings took
place at Execution Dock, on the Thames River at
Wapping, where a gallows was set up on the mud
at low tide. The corpse was left until three
tides had washed over it and then
displayed in an iron cage, hanging
from a wooden frame called a gibbet.

"Farewell to young and old,
all jolly seamen bold,
You're welcome to my gold,
for I must die,
I must die."

Captain Kid's Farewell
A song printed to be sold at his execution in 1701

> ADMIRALTY—*the branch of a government that is responsible for the Navy and crimes committed at sea*

A sticky end

After the execution, the pirate's corpse was covered with tar and left to hang from a gibbet, farther down the Thames River. Captain Kidd's gibbeted corpse lasted for 20 years, gradually falling to pieces—warning passing sailors of the fate awaiting those who turned pirate.

On trial

British pirates were tried by the High Court of the Admiralty, in the Old Bailey, London, as shown here. Trials rarely lasted more than two days, with as many as 30 tried together. The accused had to defend themselves, which was not easy for uneducated seamen.

Execution

A hanging at Execution Dock was popular public entertainment. People watched from the shore and from boats, and the condemned often made a final speech. The rope was a short one, and victims died a slow death from strangulation, rather than from a broken neck. The hangman sometimes pulled on their legs, to shorten their suffering.

❯ Captain Kidd was hanged twice, as the rope broke on the first attempt.

*pirate junks
in flames*

*junks of the
Imperial Navy*

*naval troops in
blue uniforms,
armed with bows*

Fighting the pirates

This beautiful painting on silk shows the Chinese Imperial Navy fighting—and winning—a battle against the pirate fleet. Unlike the scene shown in this painting, the pirates usually won such battles, for they had many more junks than the government did. The menace of the pirates only ended, in 1810, when the Chinese emperor offered them an amnesty, which Madam Cheng accepted.

Junks

The Chinese have sailed junks, such as this modern example, for more than 2,000 years. A junk's sails are stiffened by thin strips of wood, allowing them to be placed at different angles to catch the wind.

CHINESE PIRATES

The most powerful pirate fleet in history sailed the South China Sea, between 1805 and 1810. It was called the Red Flag Fleet, and it was commanded by a pirate named Cheng Yi. When he died in 1807, his widow, known to us as Madam Cheng, took over the leadership. With several hundred large wooden ships, called junks, the pirate fleet was bigger than many navies of the time. The pirates seized merchant ships and fishing vessels and raided coastal settlements. The Chinese Imperial Navy could not defeat them.

Up the Pearl River

This is the great Pearl River of southern China. In 1808–1809, the pirate fleet sailed up the river, deep inland, looting villages. They forced the villagers to pay tribute (gifts of money or valuables) in order to be left in peace.

 > In April 1810, 17,318 pirates accepted an amnesty, handing over 226 junks to the government.

Pirate junks have lighter sails and fly long, narrow flags.

A long sword was also used, if necessary.

◉ THE PIRATE QUEEN

Madame Cheng, overall commander of the Red Flag Fleet, was a strong leader. She drew up a set of rules punishing with beheading pirates who disobeyed orders. For lesser offenses, they could be whipped or have their ears cut off. Despite what is shown in this picture, she did not do any fighting herself. When the fleet went into battle, it was commanded by her adopted son, Chang Po Tsai, whom she later married.

British engraving of Madam Cheng

A pair of curved daggers was used as weapons.

"The pirates are many, we only few; the pirates have large vessels, we only small ones."

Admiral Tsuen Mow Sun
of the Chinese Imperial Navy, 1809

Chang Po Tsai

After accepting the amnesty agreement in 1810, Chang Po Tsai became an officer in the Imperial Navy. His job was then to hunt down other pirates. He is still remembered in China, where he appears as a hero in action movies.

DEFEAT OF THE JUNKS

In the 1840s, a new pirate fleet of 70 junks set sail in the South China Sea. Its leader, Shap Ng Tsai, captured merchant ships and forced coastal villages to give him supplies and money. The Chinese Navy was too weak to stop him. But, in 1849, Shap Ng Tsai made the mistake of seizing three merchant ships belonging to the powerful British East India Company. This led the British Navy to hunt him down.

The flag of the British East India Company combined the British Union flag, in the corner, with red and white stripes.

British naval marine

Shap Ng Tsai's flagship explodes after being hit by British shells

Surprise attack

In October 1849, a fleet of three British ships, under Commander John Hay (1821–1912), make a surprise attack on Shap Ng Tsai's fleet in Haiphong, Vietnam. The junks, caught at anchor, are no match for British warships armed with powerful cannon. The British ships, two of them steam-powered, pick off the junks one by one.

pirate from a Chinese junk

> Only six junks escaped from the battle, one of them carrying Shap Ng Tsai.

> "Shap Ng Tsai's junk blew up with a tremendous crash."

Commander John Hay
from a report on the battle

Steam power

Unlike junks, steamers could sail in any direction. The British Navy also had better guns, with exploding shells, rather than the solid cannonballs used by the Chinese. Below, another steamer, *HMS Medea*, destroys 13 pirate junks in 1850.

Chinese imperial flag, captured by the British Navy in a war against China, in 1839–1842

The junks are crowded together, making it hard to escape or fight back.

HMS Fury, a British Naval war steamer

Hit by British shells, a pirate junk sinks beneath the sea.

⊖ SOUVENIR FLAG

At the end of the battle, the British Navy had destroyed 58 pirate junks, killing more than 1,700 Chinese pirates. As a souvenir of their victory, they took this pirate flag. It is said to have belonged to Shap Ng Tsai. However, as his flagship was blown up, it is hard to see how his flag could have survived. The figure on the flag is Tien Hou, or Mazu, a goddess who calmed storms and protected seafarers.

pirate flag from the battle

http://tinyurl.com/2vln8gm

SWASHBUCKLING—describes a type of fiction filled with adventure, romance, and sword fighting

PIRATE FICTION

The most notorious pirates, such as Henry Morgan, Anne Bonny, and Blackbeard, lived between 1650 and 1720, a period known as the "golden age of piracy." Although the golden age ended, the charismatic pirates of the time were never forgotten, and their lives have inspired many stories, plays, and movies. Today, fictional pirates, such as Captain Jack Sparrow, Long John Silver, and Captain Hook, are as famous as Blackbeard.

Ships were only partly constructed for the movies. Computer imagery was used to fill in the gaps.

Captain Jack Sparrow's famous frock coat, worn throughout the movie series

Hollywood hit

In this century, pirates are still popular, thanks to *Pirates of the Caribbean*, a series of Hollywood movies starring Johnny Depp as Captain Jack Sparrow, a comic pirate who relies on his quick wits, rather than weapons, to escape from dangerous situations. Keira Knightley plays Elizabeth Swann, a respectable young lady who becomes a pirate, skilled with both sword and pistol.

Elizabeth Swann's richly embroidered pirate costume, from the third movie in the series

moviestars of *Pirates of the Caribbean*

Our idea of pirate speech, including the exclamation, "arr!", comes from Robert Newton's performance as Long John Silver.

◉ CAPTAIN BLOOD

The 1935 Hollywood movie *Captain Blood* was the first lead role for Australian actor Errol Flynn (1909–1959), who became a huge star on its release. Flynn plays Captain Peter Blood, a swashbuckling hero, forced to become a pirate after being sold into slavery. He tells his men, "It's the world against us, and us against the world!"

Errol Flynn as the legendary Captain Blood

Long John Silver

The most influential pirate story of all time is Robert Louis Stevenson's novel, *Treasure Island* (1883). Its villain is the cunning, one-legged Long John Silver. In the 1950s, English actor Robert Newton (1905–1956) played Silver in two movies and a television series.

Captain Hook

The villain of J. M. Barrie's 1904 play *Peter Pan* is Captain James Hook, a pirate with a hook for a hand. The story has been retold in many forms, including movies, cartoons, stage musicals, and pantomimes.

"Fifteen men on the
dead man's chest,
Yo-ho-ho, and a bottle of rum!
Drink and the devil had
done for the rest.
Yo-ho-ho, and a bottle of rum!"

pirate song from Robert Louis Stevenson's novel, *Treasure Island* (1883)

Singing pirates

There is a long tradition of pirate musicals and operas, beginning with *The Pirates*, a 1792 opera by the English composer Steven Storace. More recent examples are two American musicals, *The Pirate Queen* (2006) and *Blackbeard the Musical* (2008). The best known is Gilbert and Sullivan's 1879 comic opera, *The Pirates of Penzance*, still performed around the world today.

Richard, leader of the Pirates of Penzance, sings, "It is a glorious thing to be a pirate king!"

EXCAVATE—to investigate a site by digging it up

The map gives few clues to the location of the island. Many possibilities have been suggested, including the Vietnamese island of Phu Quoc.

Treasure map

In 1929, Hubert Palmer, an English collector of pirate relics, bought some chests that supposedly once belonged to Captain Kidd. He said that, inside them, he found four maps of an unidentified island. Many searchers have tried to find the island, hoping to locate Kidd's treasure. The maps are probably modern fakes.

In 1983, two treasure hunters went to Phu Quoc to search for Kidd's riches. In fact, Kidd did not sail anywhere near Vietnam.

A small selection of gold jewelry from the wreck of Black Sam Bellamy's pirate ship.

TREASURE HUNTERS

In 1701, on the night before he was hanged for piracy, Captain Kidd wrote a letter to the government offering to reveal the location of a huge treasure. This was probably a desperate bluff to delay his execution. Yet many people have tried to find Kidd's treasure and other pirates' treasures, too. So far, the only genuine pirate treasure discovered is that of Black Sam Bellamy, whose ship, *Whydah Galley*, sank in a storm off Cape Cod, Massachusetts, in 1717.

> The sand around the wreck of the *Whydah Galley* is full of gold dust, which will take years to recover.

"In my proceedings in the Indies, I have lodged goods and treasure to the value of one hundred thousand pounds."

Captain Kidd (c. 1645–1701)
from his last letter (1701)

A diver exploring the treasures from Black Sam Bellamy's ship.

Successful search

After many years searching, American underwater explorer Barry Clifford found the wreck of the *Whydah Galley* in 1983. He identified the ship by its bell, which has the vessel's name written on it.

Underwater archaeology

Barry Clifford and his team of divers spent many years scouring the seabed for pieces of the *Whydah Galley*. This was difficult work, as the finds were scattered over a wide area and buried beneath thick layers of silt. Using underwater metal detectors, the divers were able to find a huge amount of treasure.

an artifact from the *Whydah Galley*

● OAK ISLAND MONEY PIT

Some people think that Hubert Palmer's maps show Oak Island, off Nova Scotia, in Canada. In 1795, three boys discovered a mysterious, deep pit here. In the belief that it held treasure—perhaps Captain Kidd's stash—it was nicknamed the "Money Pit." Despite many attempts to excavate the pit, no treasure has ever been found inside it.

the Money Pit

GLOSSARY

amnesty
An agreement whereby a state or government offers to "forget" the crimes of a guilty person, if the guilty person agrees to stop committing the crimes.

bagno
A North African prison, used to keep slaves locked up overnight.

Barbary coast
An old European name for the north coast of Africa, named after the local people, who were called Berbers.

boarding ax
An ax used to climb on board an enemy ship.

booty
Goods seized by force, by armed forces in wartime, or by pirates and privateers.

broadside
Firing all the cannon at once, along one side of a warship.

buccaneers
The name for 17th-century pirates and privateers who attacked Spanish ships and settlements in the Caribbean.

careen
To clean the hull of a ship by tilting it on one side and scraping away seaweed, barnacles, and shipworm.

corsair
A privateer or pirate operating in the Mediterranean Sea. There were Barbary corsairs from North Africa and southern European corsairs.

cutlass
A short, curved slashing sword, used in naval warfare.

dividers
A navigational instrument with two metal arms and a hinged joint, used for measuring distances and marking a course on a map.

empire
A large area of territory, with different peoples governed by a single state.

friar
A member of a Christian brotherhood, dedicated to spreading the faith by preaching to people.

fusil boucanier
A musket with a very long barrel, used by French buccaneers.

galley
A large, single-decked ship, powered by oar and sail, used mostly in the Mediterranean.

gallows
A wooden frame used to execute (kill) criminals by hanging them by the neck from a rope.

gibbet
A wooden structure that displayed the body of an executed criminal, often suspended from it in a metal cage, to warn people not to break the law.

grappling iron
An iron tool, with several hooks, that was swung from a rope and used to grab hold of an enemy ship, to pull it close for boarding.

hold
The area on the lower deck of a ship, where cargo is stored.

janissary

A Muslim infantry soldier (or foot soldier), active in the Turkish Ottoman Empire between the 1300s and 1800s.

Jolly Roger

A pirate flag decorated with frightening images such as skulls and devils.

junk

A Chinese sailing ship, with sails stiffened by thin strips of wood called battens.

lateen

A triangular sail, set on a long yard (pole) mounted at an angle to the mast.

marine

A soldier trained to fight at sea or in seaborne operations.

maroon

To leave someone behind on a desert island or an uninhabited coast, as a punishment.

monastery

A settlement of monks—Christian holy men who take vows to spend their lives serving God.

musketeer

A foot soldier trained to use a long-barreled gun, fired from the shoulder, called a musket.

navigation

The science of finding the way at sea.

New World

The European name for the Americas, following their discovery in the later 1400s.

pieces of eight

An English nickname for Spanish silver dollar coins.

pirate

A seafarer who attacks shipping or coastal settlements illegally.

plunder

To steal goods by force. The stolen goods are also called plunder.

privateer

An individual who is given government permission to seize merchant ships and attack settlements that belong to an enemy country.

prize

A ship captured in battle by a pirate or privateer.

shell

A missile, fired from a cannon, packed with an explosive charge.

shipworm

A type of clam that fastens onto the wooden hulls of ships and bores holes in them.

sloop

A small sailing ship with one mast, a large mainsail, and one or more small foresails.

talent

An ancient Greek and Roman measurement of weight. A Roman talent was the same as 71.7 lb. (32.5kg).

tavern

An inn or public house where alcoholic drinks, such as rum, were sold.

Viking

A sea raider from Scandinavia, active between the 700s and 1000s.

INDEX

INVESTIGATE

Find out how experts know about pirates and explore history
by checking out books, museums, and websites. Enjoy, me hearties!

An illustration from Howard Pyle's
Book of Pirates (1921)

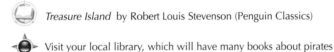

Written sources

Read books about pirates to learn more about how they lived. Compare real-life pirates with fictional ones such as Long John Silver in *Treasure Island*.

◍ *Treasure Island* by Robert Louis Stevenson (Penguin Classics)

◈ Visit your local library, which will have many books about pirates

These Somali pirates are raising their arms to show that they surrender.

http://memory.loc.gov

Pirates in the news

Look out for news stories of recent pirate attacks. The quickest way to find these is by searching on the Internet—for example, the Google website news page or the AOL news site.

Visitors can experience what life was like on board the famous *Golden Hinde*

◍ *Pirates of the 21st century* by Nigel Cawthorne (John Blake)

◈ Paley Center for Media, New York, NY 10019

www.aol.com

Replica ships

There are several museum ships you can visit, including two replicas of Sir Francis Drake's ship, the *Golden Hinde*. You can go on board both ships and explore the decks and cabins.

At the Viking Ship Museum in Roskilde, Denmark, replica ships are on display

◍ *The Great Expedition: Sir Francis Drake on the Spanish Main* by Angus Konstam (Osprey Publishing)

◈ The *USS Niagara*, Erie Maritime Museum, Erie, PA 16507

www.flagshipniagara.org

Maritime museums

Around the world, there are many maritime museums where you can learn about the history of life at sea. These often have special exhibitions on piracy.

◍ *Real Pirates: The Untold Story of the Whydah* by Barry Clifford (National Geographic Children's Books)

◈ Mystic Seaport: The Museum of America and the Sea, Greenmanville Avenue, Mystic, CT 06355

www.councilofamericanmaritimemuseums.org